Keira & Me

By Marsay

Illustrated By Brittany Jackson

Yasram Global Industries, United States

Keira & Me – Homonyms & Homophones

Illustrator: Brittany Jackson

Cover Design: Brittany Jackson

Publisher: Yasram Global Industries, LLC
Grand Blanc, MI

ISBN-13:978-0692365021 (Yasram Global Industries, LLC)
ISBN-10:0692365028

Library of Congress Control Number: 2015904610

Published & Printed in the United States of America

Dedication

To Uncle Jimmy

There are many things that I have accomplished in life, and, of the two most significant accomplishments, you have always been present with your support. Thank you for your faith in me as I worked diligently over the years to create Keira & Me. Your dedication will be greatly rewarded.

Love
Marsay

Keira & Me

Homonyms and Homophones

YumYum
Cotton Topped Tamarin
from Colombia

San
Red Belly Monkey
from Nigeria

Big Dee
Monk Seal
from United States

TJ
Polar Bear
from Russia

Weesie
Prairie Dog
from Mexico

Plunk
Three Toed Sloth
from Brazil

Ook
Black Elephant
from South Africa

Pup
Panda Bear
from China

Good morning, Keira, time for school.

Auntie Marsay, what will you teach in class today?

Well, Keira, today you and the students will learn about Homonyms and Homophones.

1

2

A Homonym
is a single word
that has
different meanings,
but the word sounds
the same each
time you use it.

Homophones are words
that sound alike,
but they are spelled
differently and have
different meanings.

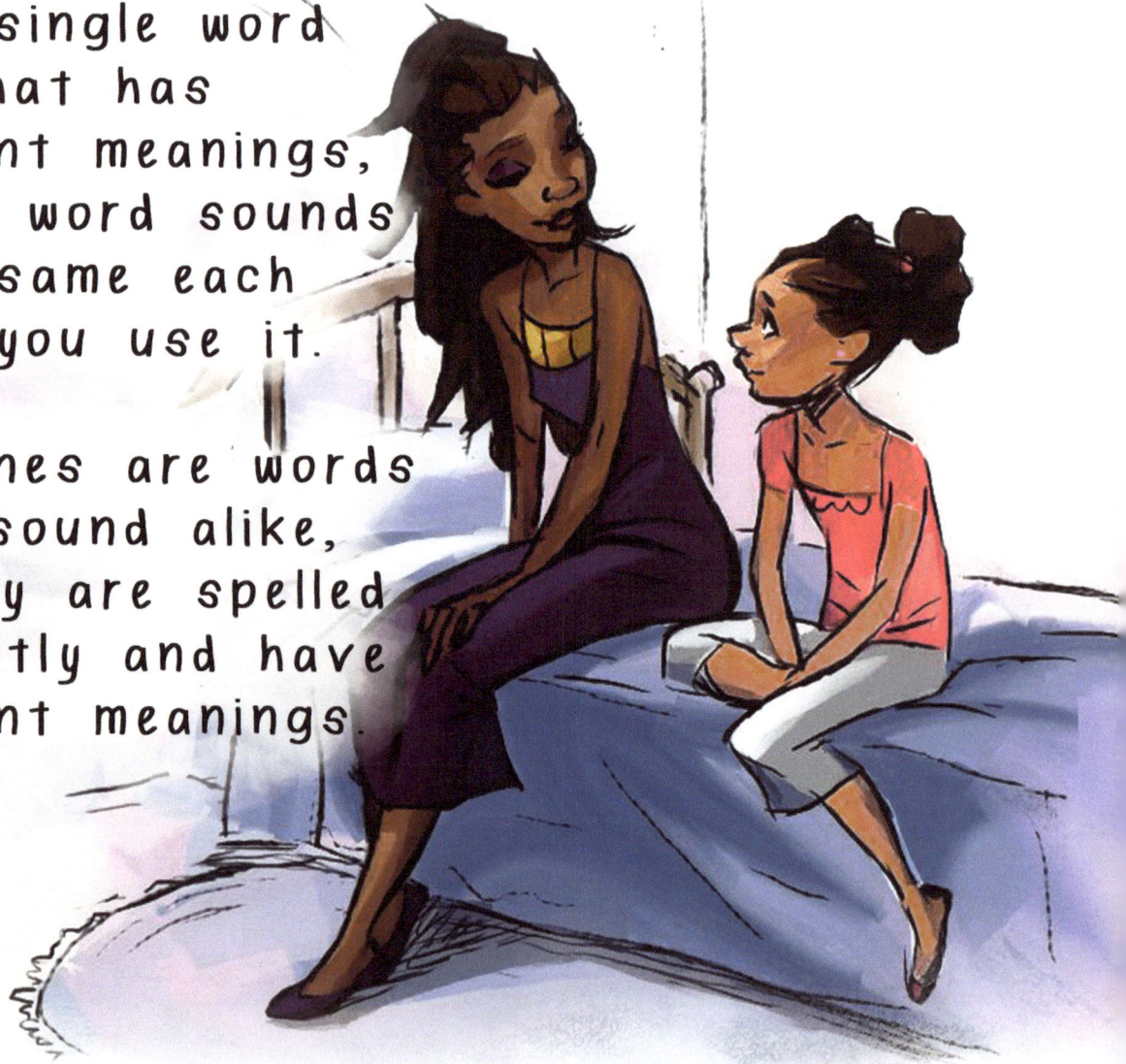

That sounds confusing!

no, Keira, Homonyms and Homophones can both be a lot of fun when you understand them.

We use them every day, and we never know when we're using them until we write them in a sentence. I'll explain more in class today.

Yeah, man, it was really cool! This weekend, Plunk, Tj, and I worked together to add words to the beat for a new song.

We'll play it for you during band practice after school.

I sent the beat to Weesee, so she can add more of her fancy guitar rifts!

Yeah, guys, you're really going to love my cool new sound.

8

Hello, class!

How was your weekend?

My family and I went to visit my grandparents in Costa Rica.

Where is Costa Rica?

Costa Rica
is located here
in Central America.

Yum Yum,
I thought you
visited your family?

Yes, Keira,
Abuela is Spanish
for grandmother
and Abuelo is Spanish
for grandfather.

Ok, class, today you will learn how to use Homonyms and Homophones correctly in a sentence.

Class-

Home-on-thems
and Home-on-the-phone?

No, class! Keira will you please explain to the class what they are?

A Homonym is a single word that is spelled the same way, but it has different meanings, and the word sounds the same each time you use it.

Homophones are words that sound alike, but they are spelled differently and have different meanings.

Very good, Keira!
We use them
both everyday,
and we never
know until we
have to
spell them.

It's important,
when we are
writing sentences,
that we use
each word
correctly.
for example:

The tree bark
is brown.

Did the dog bark
at me?

This is
an example
of a Homonym.

I understand,
Ms. Marsay.
A tree has bark,
and a dog can bark!

Very good, San!
Now here is an example
of a Homophone?

We <u>eight</u>
pizza for dinner
last night.

Ms. Marsay,
you can't eight a pizza.
That eight is how
we spell the number 8.

Good, Weesee!
So, who can tell me
the correct way
to spell eight
for this sentence?

Excellent, Ook!

Ate and eight
are Homophones.

This sounds cool!
Can I try?

A wonderful Homonym, Tj!

He stepped in
the p<u>ool</u> of water.

I like to play p<u>ool</u>
with my dad.

I have one!

I did not break the plate.

Dad stepped on the car brake.

29

Great Homophone,
Big Dee!

30

The sun is
beautiful outside.

My mother has
a son named Pup.

How about this?

Your mother
has a smart
son, Pup!

For homework tonight, I would like for each of you to create a list of 10 Homonyms or Homophones.

We will review them tomorrow in class. Class is dismissed!

Hey, Pup,
I know you and some of
the guys over the weekend
tried adding words to
Big Dee's beat.

How about we write a song
together using Homophones?
We can sing it in
class tomorrow for
Ms. Marsay.

That's an awesome idea!

34

Yes, Auntie Marsay. The class worked together as a team to write a Homophone song just for you.

Hit It!!

Hey, I don't mean <u>hay</u> that's for cows. Did you <u>see</u> me standing by the deep blue <u>sea</u>?

When we win I will sing this song over! Boy, did I <u>wail</u> when my eyes saw the big gray <u>whale</u>!

I'll say good <u>night</u> to the
tall pale <u>knight</u>, for they <u>reign</u>
in the castle where the
<u>rain</u> fills my pail!

This song has <u>won</u>,
for the
Sally Court Club
is number <u>one</u>!

I must say, I am proud of each one of you. You really know your Homophones! Did you forget about Homonyms?

Sorry, Ms. Marsay!
We were having so much fun
with Homophones that we forgot
about the Homonyms.

That's ok, class, but remember,
Homonyms are words
that are spelled the same way
and have the same sound but
have different meanings.
Homophones are words
that sound alike,
have different meanings,
and are spelled differently.

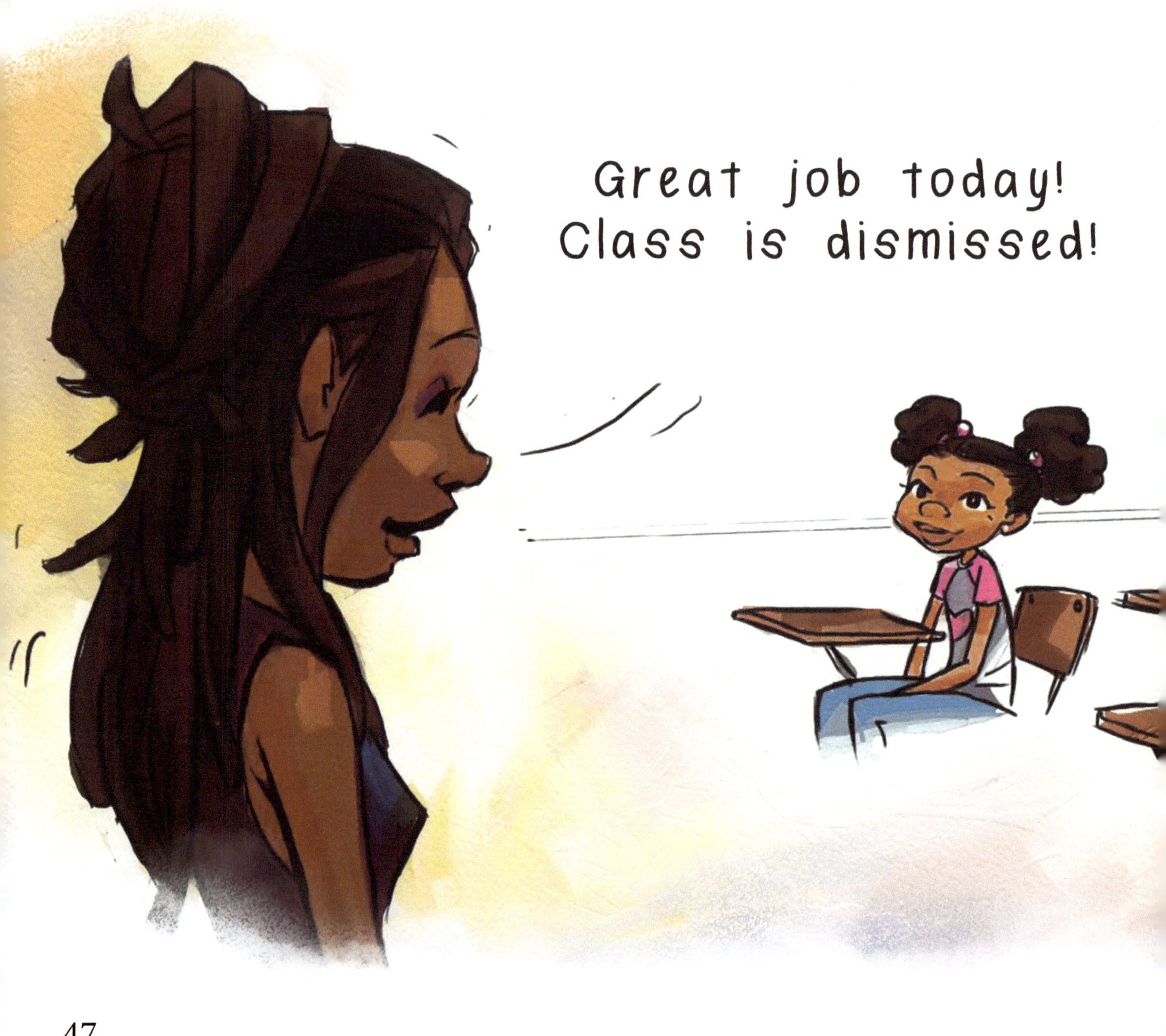
Great job today!
Class is dismissed!

About the Author

Marsay Wells-Strozier, is the founder of the not-for-profit organization, Center for Higher Educational Achievement (CHEA), and the for-profit company, Yasram Global Industries, LLC. She is completing her Doctorate Degree (Ed.D.) from Walden University in Administrator Leadership for Teaching & Learning, Boston, MA. She holds a Master of Arts Degree in Education & Instruction (M.A. Ed.) and a Master of Science Administration Certificate in General Administration (M.S.A.), both from Central Michigan University, Mt. Pleasant, MI, and also a Bachelor of Business Administration Degree (B.B.A.) from Baker College, Flint, MI.

Marsay has devoted 15 years of her professional career educating children and adults in Flint and Detroit, MI. Through her not-for-profit organization (CHEA), she seeks to help families put the puzzle of life together by providing: uniquely structured adult education and job training programs, workshops, low income housing, and affordable performing arts programs for low income children. She is a contributing editor to Examiner.com on Urban Education and also the founder of the Genesee County Master Mind Group. Her personal goal is to touch and inspire individuals to lead a more knowledgeable and happier life by acquiring the desire for lifelong learning through education, mentoring, and training.

www.ingramcontent.com/pod-product-compliance
Lightning Source LLC
Chambersburg PA
CBHW041426090426
42741CB00002B/54